PRAYERS THE DEVIL HATES

BOOK 2

MIRACLES

30 Days of Miracle Prayers, Devotions, and
Declarations to Transform Your Life

PRAYER FOUNTAIN
Joe & Nicole Wood

Prayers The Devil Hates: MIRACLES

30 Days of Miracle Prayers, Devotions, and Declarations To Transform Your Life

Copyright © 2023 Joe & Nicole Wood

Published by The Prayer Fountain
9835 Lake Worth Rd STE 16 #145
Lake Worth, FL 33467

www.PrayerFountain.com

ISBN: 9798859286614

First Edition: 2023

For inquiries about bulk purchases, special sales, or corporate premium sales, please contact us via our website www.PrayerFountain.com.

Unless otherwise indicated, all Scripture quotations are taken from the Holy Bible, New Living Translation, copyright © 1996, 2004, 2015 by Tyndale House Foundation. Used by permission of Tyndale House Publishers, Inc., Carol Stream, Illinois 60188. All rights reserved.

DAY 1

THE WONDER OF CREATION

Genesis 1:1 - *In the beginning God created the heavens and the earth.*

GOD SPEAK TO ME

Take a moment to ponder the vastness and beauty of creation. Ask God to open your eyes to see His handiwork in everything around you, revealing His power and love.

DEVOTIONAL

The very first line of the Bible introduces us to a God of immense power and creativity. It's a simple yet profound statement that shapes our understanding of everything else we encounter in Scripture and in life. Before there was anything, there was God, and from His will and word, everything came into being.

From the expansive galaxies to the minute details of the cellular world, God's creativity is evident. Each sunrise and sunset, every mountain peak and ocean depth, shouts of His splendor. The universe is not just a random occurrence but a deliberate act of God, and within it, He carefully fashioned humanity in His image.

When we truly grasp the magnificence of creation, it draws us into a deeper worship of the Creator. We are reminded that the same God who brought forth the universe desires a relationship with us. The vastness of the cosmos only amplifies the depth of His love for each individual.

SCRIPTURES TO READ

Psalm 19:1-4; Romans 1:20; Nehemiah 9:6; Colossians 1:16-17

PRAYER OF RESPONSE

Dear Heavenly Father, I stand in awe of Your marvelous works. Every star, every creature, every breath of wind testifies to Your greatness. Thank you for the reminder that in Your grand design, You still know and care for me intimately. Help me to see Your hand in every detail of my life and to worship You with profound gratitude. Let my life be a testament to Your love and creativity. In Jesus' name, I pray. Amen.

SO WHAT? WHO CARES? HOW DOES THIS APPLY TO ME?

When was the last time you paused to marvel at creation? Describe that moment.

_____

_____

How does understanding God as the Creator of the universe shape your view of Him in your personal life?

_____

_____

What part of creation speaks most profoundly to you about God's character? Why?

_____

_____

How can you cultivate a greater appreciation for God's creation in your daily routine?

_____

_____

Who can you share the wonder of God's creation with this week?

_____

_____

DECLARATION

I am a cherished part of God's grand design.

The Creator of the universe knows me intimately and loves me deeply.

Every day, I will recognize and rejoice in God's handiwork around me.

I am fearfully and wonderfully made, crafted with purpose by the Master's hand.

DAY 2

THE PROMISE IN THE STORM

Genesis 6:9 - *This is the account of Noah and his family. Noah was a righteous man, the only blameless person living on earth at the time, and he walked in close fellowship with God.*

GOD SPEAK TO ME

Ask God to strengthen your resolve in challenging times and to help you remain faithful to His call. Open your heart and mind to hear what God has to say to you today.

DEVOTIONAL

In a world consumed by wickedness, Noah stood out as a beacon of faithfulness. The Earth was filled with violence, yet in the midst of it all, Noah was a testament to what it meant to walk in close fellowship with God. Such was his righteousness that God entrusted him with a monumental task: to build an ark and preserve the remnants of creation during a global flood.

Imagine the ridicule Noah faced, the doubters and mockers who questioned his sanity. Yet, his trust in God never wavered. He acted on God's instruction, not swayed by the opinion of man. The floodwaters eventually came, cleansing the Earth, but God's promise prevailed. Noah and his family emerged from the ark to a renewed world, complete with a rainbow – a sign of God's everlasting covenant and mercy.

Noah's story is more than a tale of an ark and animals. It's a reminder that in a world that often feels chaotic and contrary to God's ways, He is always in control. God honors those who trust in Him, even when it seems irrational to the world.

SCRIPTURES TO READ

Genesis 6:14-22; Genesis 9:12-16; Hebrews 11:7; 2 Peter 2:5

PRAYER OF RESPONSE

Dear Heavenly Father, like Noah, let my faith in You be unwavering even when the world does not understand. Strengthen my resolve to obey Your call, no matter how challenging it may seem. Remind me of Your promises, especially when the storms of life rage. Help me to be a beacon of hope and trust in a world that often forgets You. In Jesus' name, I pray. Amen.

SO WHAT? WHO CARES? HOW DOES THIS APPLY TO ME?

How do you respond when God's directives conflict with worldly perspectives?

_____

_____

In what areas of your life do you need to trust God more fully?

_____

_____

What promises of God are you holding onto in your current season of life?

_____

_____

How can you emulate Noah's unwavering faith in your community?

_____

_____

Who can you share the story of Noah's faith and God's promises with this week?

_____

_____

DECLARATION

I am grounded in God's promises and directed by His word.

Though the world may mock, my faith in God will remain steadfast.

God's promises are sure, and His mercy endures forever.

I am a vessel of hope and trust in a world seeking direction.

DAY 3

GOD'S PATH THROUGH THE IMPOSSIBLE

Exodus 14:21-22 - *Then Moses raised his hand over the sea, and the LORD opened up a path through the water with a strong east wind. The wind blew all that night, turning the seabed into dry land. So the people of Israel walked through the middle of the sea on dry ground, with walls of water on each side!*

GOD SPEAK TO ME

Ask God to reveal His power and guidance, even when faced with the seemingly impossible. Open your heart and mind to hear what God has to say to you today.

DEVOTIONAL

The Israelites, having been freed from Egyptian bondage, found themselves trapped between the mighty Egyptian army and the vast Red Sea. To the human eye, their situation seemed dire, with no way out. Yet, in that moment of great peril, God demonstrated His unparalleled power.

God used Moses as an instrument to part the Red Sea, providing a way out for His people and ensuring their deliverance. This awe-inspiring miracle reminds us that no matter how insurmountable our problems may seem, God has the ability to create a path where none exists.

In our lives, we will encounter "Red Sea moments" - situations where we feel cornered, with the weight of the world closing in. Yet, just as He did for the Israelites, God can make a way for us. When we trust Him wholeheartedly and obey His commands, we'll witness His miraculous power in action.

SCRIPTURES TO READ

Exodus 14:13-31; Psalm 77:16-20; Isaiah 43:16-19

PRAYER OF RESPONSE

Dear Heavenly Father, in times of despair and uncertainty, help me remember the miraculous way You parted the Red Sea. Increase my faith to trust in Your unmatched power, especially when faced with overwhelming challenges. As I navigate life's trials, guide my steps and make a way where there seems to be none. May I always praise and glorify You for Your never-ending faithfulness. In Jesus' name, I pray. Amen.

SO WHAT? WHO CARES? HOW DOES THIS APPLY TO ME?

What are the "Red Sea moments" you have faced or are facing in your life?

_____

_____

How can you better trust God when confronted with challenging situations?

_____

_____

Recall a time when God made a way for you when it seemed impossible.

_____

_____

How can you encourage someone in your life who is currently facing their own "Red Sea moment"?

_____

_____

What steps can you take to strengthen your faith and reliance on God's power?

_____

_____

DECLARATION

I am led by a God who parts seas and conquers armies.

My faith is anchored in the One who turns impossibilities into pathways of deliverance.

When faced with adversity, I will stand firm, knowing God will make a way.

I am a testament to God's power and His promise to never forsake His own.

DAY 4

ENCOUNTER WITH THE DIVINE

Exodus 3:2-3 - *There the angel of the LORD appeared to him in a blazing fire from the middle of a bush. Moses stared in amazement. Though the bush was engulfed in flames, it didn't burn up. 'This is amazing,' Moses said to himself. 'Why isn't that bush burning up? I must go see it.'*

GOD SPEAK TO ME

Pause and consider the moments when God has tried to get your attention or spoken to you in unexpected ways. Ask Him to open your eyes and ears to His callings, even in the midst of the ordinary.

DEVOTIONAL

In the mundane rhythm of tending sheep, Moses encountered the divine. A bush, ordinary in every sense, was set ablaze but not consumed. This supernatural occurrence was God's chosen method to call Moses into a divine mandate.

The burning bush serves as a profound reminder that God can speak to us in the most unexpected places. He can transform the ordinary into the extraordinary, drawing us closer to His purpose. Moses' encounter changed the trajectory of his life and the fate of the Israelites. It was more than a spectacle; it was a divine summons.

Likewise, God seeks to encounter us in our everyday lives. He desires to draw our attention, to ignite our passions, and to guide us into His will. We must be attentive, like Moses, recognizing these divine intersections and being willing to say, "Here I am."

SCRIPTURES TO READ

Exodus 3:1-15; Acts 7:30-35; Isaiah 6:8

PRAYER OF RESPONSE

Dear Heavenly Father, thank You for seeking to encounter me in the midst of my daily life. Help me to be attentive to Your voice and the ways You reveal Yourself. Give me a heart eager to respond to Your call, just as Moses did at the burning bush. Whenever You beckon, may I confidently say, "Here I am, Lord." Use me for Your glory, and let Your presence be a continual flame in my heart, guiding and illuminating my path. In Jesus' name, I pray. Amen.

SO WHAT? WHO CARES? HOW DOES THIS APPLY TO ME?

Have you ever felt God speaking to you or drawing your attention in unexpected ways? Describe that experience.

_____

_____

How can you cultivate a heart that is more receptive to God's callings?

_____

_____

Recall a time when following God's guidance led to unexpected blessings or growth in your life.

_____

_____

What steps can you take to ensure you're responsive to God's call, regardless of where it leads?

_____

_____

How can you encourage others to be attentive to God's voice in their lives?

_____

_____

DECLARATION

I am attuned to the voice of God, ever eager to respond to His call.

In the ordinary moments of life, I remain expectant of divine encounters.

Guided by His presence, my heart is set ablaze with passion and purpose.

I am ready to heed His summons and fulfill His divine mandate in my life.

DAY 5

WALLS THAT CRUMBLE

Joshua 6:20 - *When the people heard the sound of the rams' horns, they shouted as loud as they could. Suddenly, the walls of Jericho collapsed, and the Israelites charged straight into the town and captured it.*

GOD SPEAK TO ME

In your moments of reflection, consider the walls or barriers in your life that seem insurmountable. Ask God for the faith and strategy to overcome them.

DEVOTIONAL

The mighty walls of Jericho were not just physical barriers but also symbols of impossibility, mocking the Israelites' faith and hope. Yet, with a divine strategy that defied human understanding, God brought those formidable walls down.

Often in life, we are faced with our own "walls of Jericho" – challenges that seem insurmountable, barriers that hinder progress, or situations that seem impossible to navigate. But the story of Jericho reminds us that with God, all things are possible. Our part is to listen, obey, and walk in faith.

The Israelites could have doubted the unusual battle plan God provided. Marching, blowing trumpets, and shouting were unconventional methods to breach fortified walls. Yet, they trusted and obeyed, and the impossible happened.

Similarly, God may guide us in ways that don't align with worldly wisdom. It's in these moments of complete reliance on Him that miracles unfold. Whether it's a relational barrier, a financial challenge, or a personal struggle, God can and will make walls crumble when we put our faith in Him.

SCRIPTURES TO READ

Joshua 6:1-27; Hebrews 11:30; 2 Corinthians 5:7

PRAYER OF RESPONSE

Dear Heavenly Father, the Conqueror of impossibilities, I bring before You the "walls" in my life that seem unyielding. I ask for faith to trust Your strategies, even when they defy human understanding. Help me to walk in obedience, knowing that with You, every barrier can be overcome. Strengthen my resolve, fortify my trust, and let me witness the miraculous in my life. In the name of Jesus, who makes all things possible, I pray. Amen.

SO WHAT? WHO CARES? HOW DOES THIS APPLY TO ME?

What are the "walls of Jericho" in your life currently?

_____

_____

How can you actively trust God's strategies, even if they seem unconventional or challenging?

_____

_____

Recall a time when God made a way for you in a seemingly impossible situation.

_____

_____

How can you encourage others to trust in God's plan, even when faced with great obstacles?

_____

_____

In what ways can you foster a deeper faith and reliance on God during uncertain times?

_____

_____

DECLARATION

I believe in a God who makes walls crumble and pathways clear.

In the face of challenges, my faith remains unshaken, knowing God is by my side.

Guided by divine strategy, I move forward, ready to witness the miraculous.

My trust is in the Lord, who turns impossibilities into testimonies of His greatness.

Through it, I am anchored in truth and empowered to live a life pleasing to God.

DAY 6

WHEN THE SUN STOOD STILL

Joshua 10:13 - *So the sun stood still and the moon stayed in place until the nation of Israel had defeated its enemies.*

GOD SPEAK TO ME

Start by asking God to help you handle life's challenges. Open your heart and mind to hear what God has to say to you today.

DEVOTIONAL

The narrative of the sun standing still is a profound testament to God's power over creation and His commitment to His people. When Joshua and the Israelites needed more time to achieve victory, God didn't just grant them a strategic advantage or send reinforcements. He did the unimaginable - He made the sun stand still.

Life often feels like a race against the clock, with challenges pressing us from every side. Sometimes, we desperately wish for a momentary pause, a breather, or more hours in the day to navigate our battles. While God might not make the sun stand still for us literally, this account assures us of His sovereign power to intervene in our situations in ways we can't fathom.

God is not bound by the natural laws He set in place. He can, and often does, operate beyond them for the sake of His children. Our role is to trust, even when the odds seem stacked against us, and to pray bold prayers, believing that the God of Joshua is our God too.

SCRIPTURES TO READ

Joshua 10:1-15; Isaiah 38:7-8; Psalm 89:36-37

PRAYER OF RESPONSE

Dear Heavenly Father, who commands even the sun and moon, I stand in awe of Your power and grace. In the midst of life's battles, remind me that nothing is too hard for You. Increase my faith to pray audacious prayers and trust You for miraculous outcomes. Let my heart be assured that time, circumstances, and elements are under Your sovereign control. In the unwavering name of Jesus, I pray. Amen.

SO WHAT? WHO CARES? HOW DOES THIS APPLY TO ME?

Have there been instances where you've seen God's timely intervention in your life?

_____

_____

What challenges are you currently facing that seem insurmountable due to time constraints or pressures?

_____

_____

How can you lean into God's sovereignty and trust His timing, even when things seem out of control?

_____

_____

Reflect on how the knowledge of God's control over time can impact your daily decisions and perspectives.

_____

_____

What bold prayers can you start praying today, fully trusting in God's power and promises?

_____

_____

DECLARATION

I serve a God who is above time and controls every element of creation.

With Him, nothing is impossible, and every challenge is surmountable.

In every battle, I trust His timing and sovereign intervention.

I am confident in His power, knowing He can move in ways beyond comprehension.

DAY 7

ELIJAH AND THE WIDOW'S OIL

1 Kings 17:16 - *There was always enough flour and olive oil left in the containers, just as the LORD had promised through Elijah.*

GOD SPEAK TO ME

Start by asking God for the faith to trust in His promises, even when the situation looks dire. Open your heart and mind to hear what God has to say to you today.

DEVOTIONAL

In a time of drought and famine, a widow and her son were on the brink of starvation. With just a handful of flour and a bit of oil, they prepared for their last meal, believing the end was near. However, God had other plans.

Elijah, directed by the Lord, encounters this widow and asks for a small cake. It might seem unreasonable for the prophet to request the last bit of food from a starving woman. Yet, in this act of faith and obedience, God performs a miracle. The flour and oil did not run out. Every day, they had just enough.

This story reminds us that God's provision often comes in moments of surrender and obedience. It might not be an overflowing abundance that fills storehouses; sometimes, it's just enough for the day, teaching us daily dependence on Him.

In our lives, we might face moments where our resources—be it time, finances, energy, or hope—feel like they're running out. But remember, the God who ensured the widow's jar of oil didn't run dry is the same God watching over us. He asks for our faith, our surrender, and in return, promises His unfailing provision.

SCRIPTURES TO READ

1 Kings 17:7-16; Matthew 6:31-33; Philippians 4:19

PRAYER OF RESPONSE

Dear Heavenly Father, Your provision is perfect, timely, and always sufficient. In times when I'm overwhelmed by my circumstances, help me to trust in Your promises. Teach me to live in daily dependence on You, knowing that You will supply all my needs. Grow my faith, and let me see Your miraculous provision in my life. I surrender my anxieties and uncertainties to You. In Jesus' name, I pray. Amen.

SO WHAT? WHO CARES? HOW DOES THIS APPLY TO ME?

Can you recall a time when God provided for you in an unexpected or miraculous way?

_____

_____

What are the areas in your life where you're struggling to trust God's provision?

_____

_____

How can you practice daily dependence on God, especially in times of scarcity or uncertainty?

_____

_____

Reflect on the significance of the widow's act of faith and obedience. How can you emulate such faith in your own life?

_____

_____

What steps can you take to cultivate a heart that trusts in God's provision, no matter the circumstance?

_____

_____

DECLARATION

My God is Jehovah Jireh, my Provider.

In moments of scarcity, I will trust in His abundance.

Daily, He sustains me, meeting all my needs according to His riches.

I will walk in faith, knowing that He is faithful to His promises.

DAY 8

DANIEL IN THE LION'S DEN

Daniel 6:22 - *My God sent his angel to shut the lions' mouths so that they would not hurt me, for I have been found innocent in his sight. And I have not wronged you, Your Majesty.*

GOD SPEAK TO ME

Start by asking God to give you courage to stand firm in your convictions. Open your heart and mind to hear what God has to say to you today.

DEVOTIONAL

Daniel, an exemplary servant of the King, found himself in a treacherous plot fueled by jealousy. Even with the knowledge that prayer to any god or man other than King Darius would result in a death sentence inside a lion's den, Daniel remained steadfast in his devotion to the Lord.

He could have conformed, even just briefly, to save his life. But Daniel chose faith over fear. That night, in the lion's den, he was not alone. God sent His angel to close the mouths of the lions, delivering Daniel from certain death.

This miraculous account serves as a potent reminder of God's protection and the power of unwavering faith. Daniel's commitment to prayer and trust in God didn't just save him; it became a testimony of God's power and sovereignty to a pagan king and an entire empire.

As we navigate the challenges of life, we might face moments where our convictions, beliefs, or faith could put us in seemingly perilous situations.

But, just as He was with Daniel, God promises to be with us, providing the strength and courage we need.

SCRIPTURES TO READ

Daniel 6:10-24; Isaiah 41:10; Psalm 91:1-2, 14-16

PRAYER OF RESPONSE

Dear Heavenly Father, Your power and faithfulness are unmatched. Like Daniel, let my trust in You be unshakable, even when faced with life's most intimidating challenges. Strengthen my resolve to live out my convictions, knowing that You are always by my side, ready to protect and deliver me. May my life serve as a testament to Your unwavering love and power. In Jesus' name, I pray. Amen.

SO WHAT? WHO CARES? HOW DOES THIS APPLY TO ME?

Reflect on a time when you stood up for your beliefs or convictions, despite opposition or challenges. How did you feel, and what was the outcome?

_____

_____

In what areas of your life do you feel the pressure to conform, even if it goes against your values or beliefs?

_____

_____

How can you emulate Daniel's unwavering faith and trust in God, especially in challenging situations?

_____

_____

What practices or habits can you incorporate into your daily life to strengthen your faith and connection with God?

_____

_____

How can you encourage others around you to stand firm in their faith and convictions, especially when facing adversity?

_____

_____

DECLARATION

I am shielded by the Most High, even in the face of great danger.

With unwavering faith, I will stand firm in my convictions.

God's protection surrounds me, and His peace fills my heart.

I will be courageous, knowing that the Lord is my fortress and deliverer.

DAY 9

FIERY FURNACE

Daniel 3:25 - *"Look!" Nebuchadnezzar shouted. "I see four men, unbound, walking around in the fire unharmed! And the fourth looks like a god!"*

GOD SPEAK TO ME

Start by asking God to reassure you of His ever-present protection during your trials. Open your heart and mind to hear what God has to say to you today.

DEVOTIONAL

Shadrach, Meshach, and Abednego stood firm against King Nebuchadnezzar's decree, refusing to bow to an idol. Their unwavering faith led them to a furnace so hot that it consumed the soldiers who threw them in. Yet, within those flames, they were not alone.

Their conviction, combined with God's divine protection, ensured that not even the scent of the fire touched them. The king saw a fourth figure in the furnace, and many believe this was a pre-incarnation appearance of Jesus or an angel sent by God.

This miraculous deliverance reminds us of the protective power of faith. While we may face situations that seem insurmountable or challenges that threaten to consume us, our God is greater than any fiery trial. He walks with us through the flames, ensuring that we emerge unscathed and even stronger in our faith.

In moments of doubt, let's remember Shadrach, Meshach, and Abednego and the God who protected them. Let their story inspire us to stand firm in our faith, confident that God is with us in every trial.

SCRIPTURES TO READ

Daniel 3:13-30; Isaiah 43:2; 1 Peter 4:12-13

PRAYER OF RESPONSE

Dear Heavenly Father, thank You for Your powerful protection and presence in our lives, even in the midst of our toughest trials. Help me to stand firm in my faith, knowing that You are with me in every situation. May I always prioritize You above all else, even when faced with challenges or threats. Strengthen my faith and use every trial to refine and renew my trust in You. In Jesus' name, I pray. Amen.

SO WHAT? WHO CARES? HOW DOES THIS APPLY TO ME?

Reflect on a challenging situation where you felt God's protective presence or saw His intervention. How did it strengthen your faith?

_____

_____

Have you ever felt pressured to compromise your beliefs or values? How did you respond?

_____

_____

What can you learn from Shadrach, Meshach, and Abednego's unwavering faith and commitment to God?

_____

_____

How can you deepen your trust in God's protective presence in your life?

_____

_____

In what ways can you support and encourage others facing fiery trials in their own lives?

_____

_____

DECLARATION

I am protected and guided by the Almighty God, even amidst life's fiercest flames.

My faith remains unshaken, knowing that God is always by my side.

In the face of trials, I will stand firm, confident in God's divine protection and purpose.

God's presence in my life ensures victory over every adversity.

DAY 10

JONAH AND THE BIG FISH

Jonah 1:17 - *Now the Lord had arranged for a great fish to swallow Jonah. And Jonah was inside the fish for three days and three nights.*

GOD SPEAK TO ME

Start by asking God to grant you the wisdom to recognize His signs and the humility to obey His commands. Open your heart and mind to hear what God has to say to you today.

DEVOTIONAL

The story of Jonah is one that speaks volumes about God's mercy and the consequences of disobedience. Jonah, a prophet chosen by God, tried to flee from His presence, but no one can truly escape the gaze of the Almighty. The depth of the sea and the belly of a great fish became Jonah's place of introspection and prayer. Within the darkness of the fish's belly, Jonah realized his mistakes, repented, and pleaded for God's mercy.

This incredible tale reminds us that God's plans are always greater than ours, and running from them only delays our destiny. While Jonah's situation might seem extreme, many of us, in our own ways, try to flee from God's calling or choose our comfort over His command.

Yet, even in our disobedience, God's unyielding love and mercy shine through. Jonah was saved from the depths, and the people of Nineveh were given a chance to repent. This story shows that God's compassion isn't just for the obedient but also for those who've strayed. He patiently waits for our return, ready to embrace and use us for His glory.

SCRIPTURES TO READ

Jonah 2:1-10; Psalm 139:7-10; Luke 15:11-32; Romans 8:38-39

PRAYER OF RESPONSE

Dear Heavenly Father, thank You for Your boundless mercy and patience when I've tried to run from Your calling or chosen my way over Yours. Instill in me a heart that seeks to obey and a spirit willing to go where You lead. Remind me always of Your love, even when I feel distant or lost. In Jesus' name, I pray. Amen.

SO WHAT? WHO CARES? HOW DOES THIS APPLY TO ME?

How have you tried to escape from a situation or responsibility God placed in your path?

_____

_____

Can you recall a time when, like Jonah, you felt the consequences of running from God's plans?

_____

_____

How did you experience God's mercy and compassion in a challenging situation?

_____

_____

What can you do to ensure that you're receptive and obedient to God's call in the future?

_____

_____

How can you cultivate a daily practice of seeking God's guidance and discernment in your decisions?

_____

_____

DECLARATION

I am under the watchful eyes of God, and His plans for me are greater than my own.

Even when I stray, His mercy is unfailing.

I commit to being obedient to His call and trust in His unfathomable love and guidance.

DAY 11

FEEDING OF THE 5,000

Matthew 14:19 - *Then he told the people to sit down on the grass. Jesus took the five loaves and two fish, looked up toward heaven, and blessed them. Then, breaking the loaves into pieces, he gave the bread to the disciples, who distributed it to the people.*

GOD SPEAK TO ME

Start by asking God to help you recognize His abundant provision in seemingly scarce situations. Open your heart and mind to hear what God has to say to you today.

DEVOTIONAL

In a vast crowd of over 5,000, the situation seemed impossible. Limited resources and an overwhelming need painted a picture of inevitable failure. Yet, in that moment, Jesus turned the little they had into an abundance. This miracle serves as a powerful reminder that God can take our "not enough" and turn it into "more than enough."

We often face situations where our resources, strength, or wisdom seem insufficient. It's easy to focus on what we lack rather than recognizing the One who can multiply our little. Just as Jesus took the loaves and fish, blessed them, and fed thousands, He can take our limited offerings and use them for His glory.

By entrusting our "loaves and fish" to Him, we open the door for God to do immeasurably more than we can ask or imagine. The feeding of the 5,000 encourages us to look beyond our limitations and to see the limitless potential of God's power in our lives.

SCRIPTURES TO READ

John 6:35; Philippians 4:19; Ephesians 3:20-21; 2 Corinthians 9:8

PRAYER OF RESPONSE

Dear Heavenly Father, thank You for being the God of abundance. I recognize that even when I feel limited, You are limitless. Help me to trust You with my resources, talents, and time, knowing that You can multiply them for Your glory. May I always turn to You in moments of need, remembering the miracle of the loaves and fish. In Jesus' name, I pray. Amen.

SO WHAT? WHO CARES? HOW DOES THIS APPLY TO ME?

What situations in your life seem insurmountable due to limited resources?

_____

_____

How can you entrust your "loaves and fish" to God and seek His intervention?

_____

_____

Reflect on a time when God turned your scarcity into abundance.

_____

_____

In what areas of your life do you need to experience God's miraculous provision?

_____

_____

How can you adopt an attitude of expectancy, believing God will multiply your offering?

_____

_____

DECLARATION

I serve a God of abundance who can turn my scarcity into overflowing blessings.

I trust Him with my limited resources, knowing He will multiply them for His glory.

Today, I will look beyond my limitations and see the boundless possibilities in God's hands.

DAY 12

COIN IN THE FISH'S MOUTH

Matthew 17:27 - *"However, we don't want to offend them, so go down to the lake and throw in a line. Open the mouth of the first fish you catch, and you will find a large silver coin. Take it and pay the tax for both of us."*

GOD SPEAK TO ME

Start by asking God to guide you to unexpected solutions in times of need. Open your heart and mind to hear what God has to say to you today.

DEVOTIONAL

Miracles come in various forms, and sometimes they appear in the least expected places. The story of the coin in the fish's mouth is a vivid illustration of God's ability to provide in unconventional ways. Jesus used this event to teach a lesson about God's provision and our responsibility.

Often, we find ourselves in situations where we're uncertain about our next steps or how to meet a pressing need. It's in these moments of uncertainty that God wants us to rely on His wisdom and trust His methods, no matter how unconventional they may seem.

This miracle demonstrates that God is aware of our needs, big or small. He can use the ordinary to create the extraordinary. Our task is to remain obedient, expectant, and open to His guidance, even when His directions might seem unusual.

Today, as you reflect on this story, be reminded that God's ways are higher than ours. He can turn the everyday into a divine intervention, ensuring that every need is met according to His riches in glory.

SCRIPTURES TO READ

Philippians 4:19; Isaiah 55:8-9; Proverbs 3:5-6

PRAYER OF RESPONSE

Dear Heavenly Father,thank You for Your boundless provision. I am grateful that You care about every detail of my life, even the seemingly small concerns. Teach me to lean on Your understanding and not my own. In moments of doubt or need, help me to trust Your ways, even when they seem unconventional. Expand my faith to believe that You can turn ordinary situations into miraculous provisions. In Jesus' name, I pray. Amen.

SO WHAT? WHO CARES? HOW DOES THIS APPLY TO ME?

Have you ever experienced God's provision in an unconventional or unexpected way? Describe it.

_____

_____

In what situations do you find it challenging to trust God's methods or timing?

_____

_____

How can you remain open to God's guidance, especially when His directions seem out of the ordinary?

_____

_____

How does the story of the coin in the fish's mouth challenge or reinforce your understanding of God's provision?

_____

_____

What practical steps can you take to rely more on God's wisdom and less on your understanding?

_____

_____

DECLARATION

I trust in the God who provides in ways beyond my understanding.

Today, I will be open to His unconventional solutions, believing that He cares for my every need and works all things for my good.

DAY 13

RESURRECTION OF LAZARUS

John 11:25-26 - *Jesus told her, 'I am the resurrection and the life. Anyone who believes in me will live, even after dying.'*

GOD SPEAK TO ME

Start by asking God to deepen your understanding of His life-giving power. Open your heart and mind to hear what God has to say to you today.

DEVOTIONAL

Death is a force that many fear and see as final. However, in the story of Lazarus, we are given a vivid depiction of the resurrection power of Jesus. Lazarus had been dead for four days, and many had lost hope. Yet, Jesus, who is Life itself, stepped into this situation and showcased His dominion over death.

The resurrection of Lazarus is not just a miracle; it's a powerful testament to the identity of Jesus as the Resurrection and the Life. Beyond physical death, He can breathe life into dead dreams, hopes, relationships, and passions. Where there's despair, He brings hope; where there's brokenness, He brings restoration.

As you ponder on the story of Lazarus, remember that nothing is too hard or impossible for Jesus. No matter how dire the circumstance, when Jesus steps in, life emerges. His resurrection power is available to all who believe and call upon His name.

SCRIPTURES TO READ

Romans 8:11; 1 Corinthians 15:20-22; Ephesians 1:18-20

PRAYER OF RESPONSE

Dear Heavenly Father, I am in awe of Your resurrection power. Thank You for showing us, through Lazarus, that You have the final word over death. Breathe life into areas of my existence where hope has waned, and dreams have faded. Let Your power work within me, rekindling faith and restoring joy. I believe in You, the Resurrection and the Life, and I place my trust in Your mighty works. In Your name, I pray. Amen.

SO WHAT? WHO CARES? HOW DOES THIS APPLY TO ME?

What areas in your life seem "dead" or without hope right now?

_____

_____

How does the story of Lazarus' resurrection impact your perspective on those areas?

_____

_____

When have you witnessed the resurrection power of Jesus in your own life or in the lives of others? Describe the experience.

_____

_____

How can you lean on Jesus, the Resurrection and the Life, during challenging or seemingly hopeless times?

_____

_____

What can you do to keep the hope of Christ's resurrection power alive in your daily walk?

_____

_____

DECLARATION

I believe in the resurrection power of Jesus Christ.

Regardless of the circumstances, I will hope in Him, knowing that He can breathe life into any situation.

Today, I choose to trust in His life-giving authority and remember that He is the Resurrection and the Life.

DAY 14

NET BREAKING CATCH

Luke 5:5 - *"Master,"* Simon replied, *"we worked hard all last night and didn't catch a thing. But if you say so, I'll let the nets down again."*

GOD SPEAK TO ME

Start by asking God to deepen your trust in His provision and guidance, even when circumstances seem barren. Open your heart and mind to hear what God has to say to you today.

DEVOTIONAL

Many of us have experienced moments of toil, where we've given our best, only to come up empty-handed. It can be disheartening, leading to feelings of despair and inadequacy. Yet, the miracle of the net breaking catch of fish paints a powerful picture of God's supernatural provision even after a night of disappointment.

Simon Peter and his partners had labored all night without a catch. But at Jesus' command, they cast their nets one more time, resulting in a catch so massive that their nets began to break. This miracle wasn't just about fish; it was about faith, obedience, and God's abundance.

It's a reminder that when we step out in faith, following the Lord's leading, He can transform our situations of scarcity into ones of overflowing blessing. God can bring abundance where there was once barrenness. So, when you face discouraging situations, remember to heed Jesus' call, and you might just witness a miracle.

SCRIPTURES TO READ

Matthew 6:31-33; Philippians 4:19; Ephesians 3:20

PRAYER OF RESPONSE

Dear Heavenly Father, I am humbled by Your power and provision. Even when I've experienced disappointment and feel like giving up, remind me to trust in Your guidance and to take that next step in faith. Fill my heart with the expectancy of Your supernatural provision. I thank You for Your unwavering love and for always looking out for my best. Teach me to rely on You wholly, knowing that You can turn situations of lack into abundance. In Your name, I pray. Amen.

SO WHAT? WHO CARES? HOW DOES THIS APPLY TO ME?

When have you felt like Simon Peter, working hard with no results? Describe that situation.

_____

_____

How does the miracle of net breaking catch of fish shift your perspective on your efforts and outcomes?

_____

_____

Recall a time when you witnessed God's supernatural provision in your life. What happened?

_____

_____

How can you maintain a posture of expectancy, waiting for God's provision, even in moments of lack?

_____

_____

How can you better align your efforts with God's guidance to ensure His blessings flow into your endeavors?

_____

_____

DECLARATION

I am anchored in God's abundant provision.

Even in seasons of drought, I will remain hopeful, knowing that Jesus can bring forth blessings beyond measure.

Today, I choose to trust His guidance and remain faithful in my endeavors, expecting His hand of favor upon me.

DAY 15

HEALING THE CENTURION'S SERVANT

Matthew 8:13 - *Then Jesus said to the Roman officer, 'Go back home. Because you believed, it has happened.' And the young servant was healed that same hour.*

GOD SPEAK TO ME

Start by asking God to show you the immense power of unwavering faith, even from unexpected sources. Open your heart and mind to hear what God has to say to you today.

DEVOTIONAL

In a society where Jews and Romans typically didn't interact positively, a Roman centurion's genuine faith took Jesus by surprise. This military officer, responsible for many soldiers and possessing authority, displayed an understanding of power dynamics. He realized that just as he commanded soldiers, Jesus held authority over sickness and health.

This centurion didn't rely on his position or societal status to approach Jesus. Instead, he approached with humility and faith, believing that Jesus could heal with just a word. It's a testimony to us that true faith knows no boundaries – it isn't restricted to a specific group, ethnicity, or class. Jesus celebrates faith wherever He finds it.

How strong is your faith? Are there areas in your life where you doubt or hold back from trusting God? Let this story be an encouragement to you that with even a little faith, miracles can happen.

SCRIPTURES TO READ

Matthew 15:28; Luke 7:1-10; Hebrews 11:1; James 1:6

PRAYER OF RESPONSE

Dear Heavenly Father, I am in awe of the faith displayed by the centurion. Help me to develop such unwavering trust in You. May I believe in Your power and authority in every circumstance, knowing that You can work miracles in my life and the lives of those around me. Increase my faith, and let my life be a testimony to Your wondrous works. In Your name, I pray. Amen.

SO WHAT? WHO CARES? HOW DOES THIS APPLY TO ME?

Can you recall a time when you witnessed great faith from an unexpected source?

_____

_____

How does the centurion's approach to Jesus challenge your understanding of faith?

_____

_____

In what areas of your life are you struggling to have faith?

_____

_____

What steps can you take to strengthen your trust in God's power and promises?

_____

_____

How can you encourage someone today to trust in Jesus' authority over their situation?

_____

_____

DECLARATION

I believe in the authority of Jesus and His power to heal, deliver, and transform.

My faith is anchored in His promises, and I know that when I trust Him, miracles are possible.

I will not waver in my trust, even in challenging times.

DAY 16

THE WOMAN WHO BELIEVED A TOUCH COULD CHANGE EVERYTHING

Mark 5:34 - *And he said to her, 'Daughter, your faith has made you well. Go in peace. Your suffering is over.'*

GOD SPEAK TO ME

Start by asking God to reveal the depth of His healing power and the significance of faith that compels us to reach out to Him. Open your heart and mind to hear what God has to say to you today.

DEVOTIONAL

Among the bustling crowd, one woman, burdened with twelve years of suffering and the weight of social ostracization, believed that a mere touch of Jesus' robe would heal her. It was a quiet act, unnoticed by many but not by Jesus. In that instant, power flowed, healing was received, and her faith was acknowledged.

This narrative isn't just about physical healing but also restoration. The woman, considered unclean by society, was not just healed but also called "Daughter" by Jesus, restoring her dignity and place in society.

It reminds us that our faith, no matter how small or quiet, does not go unnoticed by God. It's a call to approach Him with boldness and belief, knowing that His love and power are available to us when we reach out in faith.

SCRIPTURES TO READ

Matthew 9:20-22; Luke 8:43-48; Psalm 107:20; Isaiah 53:5

PRAYER OF RESPONSE

Dear Heavenly Father, thank You for showing that You are not just a healer, but one who restores. I am grateful that even the smallest act of faith catches Your attention. Strengthen my faith and help me to always believe that You are just a touch away, ready to heal and restore. I commit to trusting in Your unending love and power. Amen.

SO WHAT? WHO CARES? HOW DOES THIS APPLY TO ME?

What does it mean to you that Jesus notices even the smallest acts of faith?

_____

_____

Can you identify with the woman in the story? How?

_____

_____

How does this story deepen your understanding of Jesus' compassion and power?

_____

_____

Are there areas in your life where you need healing or restoration? How can you reach out in faith to Jesus?

_____

_____

How can you encourage someone today who feels unnoticed or marginalized, based on this story?

_____

_____

DECLARATION

I believe that no act of faith is too small for God to notice.

I trust in His healing and restorative power, and I will approach Him with boldness, knowing that He cares deeply for me.

I am a valued child of God, and He is always attentive to my needs.

DAY 17

THE MASTER OF THE STORM

Mark 4:39 - *When Jesus woke up, he rebuked the wind and said to the waves, 'Silence! Be still!' Suddenly the wind stopped, and there was a great calm.*

GOD SPEAK TO ME

Start by asking God to grant you the faith to trust Him during life's tumultuous times and to recognize His sovereignty over every situation. Open your heart and mind to hear what God has to say to you today.

DEVOTIONAL

Life can sometimes feel like a violent storm, with waves crashing in from every direction, leaving us feeling overwhelmed and scared. But amid the chaos, we have a Savior who isn't daunted by the fiercest tempest.

When the disciples feared for their lives as a storm raged, they found Jesus peacefully sleeping. His calmness contrasted their panic. With a single command, Jesus demonstrated His authority over nature, turning their fear into awe.

This story reminds us that no matter how chaotic our lives get, Jesus is with us. The same voice that calmed the Sea of Galilee can bring peace to our storm-ridden hearts. We only need to call out to Him, placing our faith in His power and love.

SCRIPTURES TO READ

Matthew 8:23-27; Luke 8:22-25; Psalm 107:29; Isaiah 26:3

PRAYER OF RESPONSE

Dear Heavenly Father, thank You for being my anchor in the storm. Even when I feel overwhelmed, I know that You are beside me, guiding and protecting me. Increase my faith, Lord, so that even in the fiercest storms, I may find peace in You. Grant me the strength to trust in Your mighty power and unending love. Amen.

SO WHAT? WHO CARES? HOW DOES THIS APPLY TO ME?

How do you typically respond to the "storms" in your life?

_____

_____

What comfort do you find in knowing Jesus has power over nature and our circumstances?

_____

_____

In what situation do you currently need Jesus to say, "Silence! Be still!"?

_____

_____

How can this story shape the way you approach challenges in the future?

_____

_____

How can you extend the peace of Jesus to someone you know who is currently facing a "storm" in their life?

_____

_____

DECLARATION

In the midst of life's storms, I will not be moved, for I know Jesus is with me.

His voice that commands nature to be still will bring peace to my soul.

My faith is anchored in Him, and I trust His power and love to see me through.

DAY 18

FAITH THAT MOVES JESUS

Mark 7:29 - *Then he told her, 'For such a reply, you may go; the demon has left your daughter.'*

GOD SPEAK TO ME

Start by asking God to increase your faith, so you can boldly approach Him with your needs and challenges, confident in His love and mercy. Open your heart and mind to hear what God has to say to you today.

DEVOTIONAL

At times, our circumstances may seem insurmountable, and we might feel unworthy of approaching Jesus with our needs. The Syrophoenician woman was such a person - she wasn't an Israelite, yet she boldly approached Jesus, driven by desperation for her daughter's healing.

Jesus' initial response might seem harsh, but it served to bring out the depth of the woman's faith. She wasn't deterred. Her perseverance and belief in Jesus' power led not only to her daughter's healing but also earned her praise from the Lord.

This account teaches us about the incredible power of relentless faith. Regardless of our background or circumstances, when we approach Jesus with sincere faith, He listens. He responds. He heals.

SCRIPTURES TO READ

Mark 7:24-30; Matthew 15:21-28; Hebrews 11:6; James 1:6

PRAYER OF RESPONSE

Dear Heavenly Father, I thank You for showing me that sincere faith is recognized and honored by You. Please deepen my trust in You, and help me come to You with unshakable faith, even when faced with obstacles. Remind me that no challenge is too big for You. Amen.

SO WHAT? WHO CARES? HOW DOES THIS APPLY TO ME?

Can you recall a time when you persisted in prayer, even when it seemed like God wasn't responding? How did that situation turn out?

_____

_____

What obstacles sometimes prevent you from approaching Jesus with boldness and faith?

_____

_____

How does the Syrophoenician woman's story inspire or challenge your current understanding of faith?

_____

_____

Why do you think Jesus values persistent faith?

_____

_____

How can you encourage someone in your life to persist in their faith, especially when facing delays or challenges?

_____

_____

DECLARATION

I will approach Jesus with unwavering faith, knowing that He listens and responds to sincere hearts.

No challenge is too great, and no background too obscure for His love and mercy.

I am valued, and my faith has power in His eyes.

DAY 19

FRIENDS THAT BRING YOU TO JESUS

Mark 2:10-11 - *So I will prove to you that the Son of Man has the authority on earth to forgive sins." Then Jesus turned to the paralyzed man and said, 'Stand up, pick up your mat, and go home!"*

GOD SPEAK TO ME

Start by asking God to strengthen the bonds of friendship and community in your life, so that together, you might bring one another closer to Him. Open your heart and mind to hear what God has to say to you today.

DEVOTIONAL

The paralyzed man in Mark 2 had something invaluable: friends who were willing to go to great lengths to bring him to Jesus. Unable to get through the door, they removed part of the roof and lowered their friend to where Jesus was teaching. Their faith and determination were evident, and Jesus saw it.

Jesus didn't just address the man's physical needs but also his spiritual ones, reminding us that while our physical ailments are temporary, our souls are eternal. Through this miracle, we learn the importance of community, perseverance, and the holistic healing that Jesus offers.

The commitment of the paralyzed man's friends challenges us to reflect on our friendships. Do we have friends who would bring us t

SCRIPTURES TO READ

Mark 2:1-12; Luke 5:17-26; James 5:16; Proverbs 17:17

PRAYER OF RESPONSE

Dear Heavenly Father, thank You for the gift of friendship and community. I pray for friends who will bring me closer to You, and that I too might be such a friend to others. Help me prioritize the spiritual well-being of those around me, just as much as their physical or emotional needs. Amen.

SO WHAT? WHO CARES? HOW DOES THIS APPLY TO ME?

How does the determination of the paralyzed man's friends challenge or inspire you in your faith journey?

_____

_____

Do you have friends in your life who would go to great lengths to bring you closer to Jesus? If so, who are they?

_____

_____

How can you be more intentional about bringing friends or loved ones to experience Jesus?

_____

_____

Why is it crucial to address both spiritual and physical needs, as Jesus did in this miracle?

_____

_____

How can you strengthen the bonds of your spiritual community and encourage mutual support and faith?

_____

_____

DECLARATION

I am blessed with the gift of friendship and community.

Through the support and faith of others, I draw nearer to Jesus, and I commit to being a beacon of faith, leading others to Him as well.

DAY 20

WATER INTO WINE

John 2:11 - *This miraculous sign at Cana in Galilee was the first time Jesus revealed his glory. And his disciples believed in him.*

GOD SPEAK TO ME

Start by asking God to help you discern the deeper meaning behind His miracles and to strengthen your faith. Open your heart and mind to hear what God has to say to you today.

DEVOTIONAL

At a wedding in Cana, Jesus performed His first recorded miracle, turning water into wine. While the immediate outcome was a blessing for the wedding guests and the couple, this act bore profound spiritual symbolism. Jesus didn't just provide wine; He transformed the ordinary into the extraordinary, signifying the transformative power He brings into our lives.

Jesus uses the ordinary things and moments in our lives to demonstrate His glory and divine nature. This miracle sets the stage for all His future miracles, revealing that Jesus doesn't merely fix things but transforms them entirely. Just as water turned into the finest wine, Jesus transforms our lives from ordinary to extraordinary, from sorrow to joy, and from brokenness to wholeness.

SCRIPTURES TO READ

John 2:1-11; Isaiah 25:6-9; Ephesians 2:10

PRAYER OF RESPONSE

Dear Heavenly Father, thank You for Your transformative power. You don't just fill my needs; You exceed them, turning the mundane into miraculous. Help me to see Your hand in every area of my life and to trust in Your ability to bring beauty from ordinary situations. Amen.

SO WHAT? WHO CARES? HOW DOES THIS APPLY TO ME?

Reflect on a time when Jesus transformed an ordinary situation in your life into something extraordinary.

_____

_____

Why do you think Jesus chose a wedding as the setting for His first miracle?

_____

_____

How can this miracle inspire you to trust Jesus with the ordinary aspects of your life?

_____

_____

What "ordinary water" in your life do you wish Jesus would transform into "wine"?

_____

_____

How can you partner with God to witness and participate in transformative miracles in your community?

_____

_____

DECLARATION

I believe that Jesus is the Master of transformation, turning my ordinary moments into divine appointments.

I am open to witnessing His miraculous touch in every aspect of my life.

DAY 21

THE WITHERED HAND

Mark 3:5 - *He looked around at them angrily and was deeply saddened by their hard hearts. Then he said to the man, 'Hold out your hand.' So the man held out his hand, and it was restored!*

GOD SPEAK TO ME

Start by asking God to remove any hardness from your heart and to help you understand His compassionate nature. Open your heart and mind to hear what God has to say to you today.

DEVOTIONAL

In a synagogue, on the Sabbath, a man with a withered hand sat among the crowd. The Pharisees keenly observed Jesus, waiting to accuse Him of breaking the Sabbath laws. But Jesus, filled with compassion, chose to heal the man, challenging the religious leaders' limited perspective of what it meant to do good.

This healing wasn't just about a physical restoration, but a declaration that love and compassion should never be bound by legalism or tradition. Through this act, Jesus teaches us that human needs and compassion are always above religious rituals. While the man's hand was restored, the Pharisees' hearts remained hardened. It reminds us to always prioritize love and understanding over judgment.

SCRIPTURES TO READ

Mark 3:1-6; Micah 6:6-8; James 2:15-17

PRAYER OF RESPONSE

Dear Heavenly Father, thank You for showing me the depth of Your compassion. Help me to prioritize love over judgment and rituals. May I always have a soft heart, eager to extend Your love and healing to those in need. Amen.

SO WHAT? WHO CARES? HOW DOES THIS APPLY TO ME?

Can you recall a time when you or someone you know placed tradition or rules above compassion? How did it make you feel?

_____

_____

How can you ensure that you prioritize love and compassion in your interactions with others?

_____

_____

What traditions or habits might be hindering you from experiencing the fullness of God's compassion or showing it to others?

_____

_____

Reflect on someone you know who needs healing, whether physical, emotional, or spiritual. How can you be an instrument of God's love and healing for them?

_____

_____

How can you keep your heart soft and open to the needs of others, even when faced with challenges or opposition?

_____

_____

DECLARATION

I believe that God's compassion and love are paramount.

I will strive to prioritize these virtues in my life, ensuring that I mirror Jesus' heart in my interactions with others.

DAY 22

GRATITUDE IN THE MIDST OF MIRACLES

Luke 17:15 - *One of them, when he saw that he was healed, came back to Jesus, shouting, 'Praise God!'*

GOD SPEAK TO ME

Start by asking God to wrap His arms around you and comfort you in your time of grief. Open your heart and mind to hear what God has to say to you today.

DEVOTIONAL

Amidst the outskirts of a village, ten men stood at a distance, bound by their leprosy, cut off from society. Their desperate cries for mercy reached Jesus, and with just a word, He healed them. Yet, out of the ten, only one came back to offer gratitude.

This solitary leper's return wasn't merely about thanking Jesus; it highlighted a deep-seated recognition of who Jesus was and an understanding of grace. While all ten were physically healed, this one leper experienced a deeper, spiritual healing. His heart was transformed with gratitude.

In our lives, God continually blesses and heals us in myriad ways. This story challenges us: Are we, like the nine, so caught up in our blessings that we forget the Blessor? Or do we, like the one, come back with a heart full of gratitude?

SCRIPTURES TO READ

Luke 17:11-19; 1 Thessalonians 5:18; Psalms 107:1-2

PRAYER OF RESPONSE

Dear Heavenly Father, thank You for Your countless blessings and miracles in my life. Forgive me for the times I've taken them for granted. Fill me with a heart of gratitude that recognizes Your hand in every good thing. Amen.

SO WHAT? WHO CARES? HOW DOES THIS APPLY TO ME?

What recent blessings or miracles in your life have you possibly overlooked or taken for granted?

_____

_____

How can you cultivate a consistent attitude of gratitude in your daily life?

_____

_____

Recall a time when gratitude changed your perspective or attitude towards a situation. How did it affect your actions?

_____

_____

Why do you think gratitude is important in our relationship with God?

_____

_____

Consider ways you can express gratitude to God today. How can you also show appreciation to those around you?

_____

_____

DECLARATION

I believe that gratitude transforms hearts and minds.

I will strive to recognize and appreciate God's blessings, ensuring that I maintain a grateful heart in all circumstances.

DAY 23

PERSISTENT FAITH REVEALS CLEAR VISION

Mark 10:52 - *And Jesus said to him, 'Go, for your faith has healed you.'*
Instantly the man could see, and he followed Jesus down the road..

GOD SPEAK TO ME

Start by asking God to strengthen your faith and grant you clarity in
moments of doubt or darkness. Open your heart and mind to hear what God
has to say to you today.

DEVOTIONAL

Blind Bartimaeus sat by the roadside, a common place for beggars. But the
day Jesus passed by was unlike any other. Despite the crowd's attempt to
silence him, Bartimaeus cried out even louder, demonstrating his desperate
need and unwavering faith.

This is a story of persistent faith. Bartimaeus didn't allow his physical
blindness or the discouragement from those around him to deter his spiritual
vision. He recognized Jesus as the Messiah and firmly believed that Jesus
could restore his sight. His tenacity is a powerful lesson for us.

How many times have we allowed the 'crowd' of doubts, fears, or even
people around us to drown out our cries to Jesus? Bartimaeus teaches us to
be persistent, to keep calling out to Jesus despite the noise that tries to
silence our faith.

SCRIPTURES TO READ

Mark 10:46-52; Hebrews 11:6; Matthew 7:7-8

PRAYER OF RESPONSE

Dear Heavenly Father, thank You for showing me the power of persistent faith. Please give me the strength and resilience to keep seeking You, even when challenges try to silence my spirit. Restore clarity in areas of my life that have been blinded by doubt or fear. Amen.

SO WHAT? WHO CARES? HOW DOES THIS APPLY TO ME?

What are the 'noisy crowds' in your life that might be discouraging you from pursuing Jesus?

_____

_____

How can you exercise persistent faith in your current circumstances?

_____

_____

Recall a moment when you felt God responded to your persistent faith. How did it impact your relationship with Him?

_____

_____

In what areas of your life are you seeking clarity or healing?

_____

_____

How can you encourage someone in your life to exercise persistent faith, especially if they're going through challenging times?

_____

_____

DECLARATION

I am committed to a faith that is persistent, unyielding, and confident in the power of Jesus.

I will not let the doubts or noises of this world deter my pursuit of Christ's clarity and healing in my life.

DAY 24

DEATH CANNOT DEFEAT THE MASTER OF LIFE

Mark 5:41-42 - *Holding her hand, he said to her, 'Talitha koum,' which means 'Little girl, get up!' And the girl, who was twelve years old, immediately stood up and walked around!*

GOD SPEAK TO ME

Start by asking God to breathe life into areas of your life that may feel stagnant or dead. Open your heart and mind to hear what God has to say to you today.

DEVOTIONAL

The room was filled with mourning, the atmosphere heavy with grief. Jairus, a synagogue leader, had just lost his 12-year-old daughter. But in the midst of this despair, Jesus, the Giver of Life, walks in.

With just a simple command, "Talitha koum," Jesus raised the young girl from the dead, turning sorrow into joy, mourning into dancing. This wasn't just a display of His power but a testament to His compassion and love.

Death, be it physical or spiritual, is no match for the power of Jesus. Maybe there are parts of your life that feel 'dead' — dreams, relationships, or passions that have waned. The same Jesus who raised Jairus' daughter is available to you, ready to breathe life into every deadened part of your existence.

 Remember that God is with you in every step of the journey. He understands your pain and longs to bring healing to your marriage and family. Place your trust in His transforming power and hold onto the hope that He is able to do exceedingly abundantly above all that we ask or imagine. Allow God to guide you, heal you, and restore your relationships. With His love, forgiveness, and grace, broken marriages and families can experience redemption and become a testimony of His healing power. Trust in His promise to restore what has been broken and to bring hope to the seemingly hopeless.

SCRIPTURES TO READ

Mark 5:21-43; John 11:25-26; Romans 6:4

PRAYER OF RESPONSE

Dear Heavenly Father, You are the resurrection and the life. Breathe Your life into areas of my existence that feel devoid of hope or vigor. I trust in Your power to rejuvenate and restore. Amen.

SO WHAT? WHO CARES? HOW DOES THIS APPLY TO ME?

Are there areas in your life that feel 'dead' or stagnant? Describe them.

_____

_____

How can you invite Jesus into these areas to bring restoration and revival?

_____

_____

Reflect on a time when God brought something 'back to life' in your life. How did that experience strengthen your faith?

_____

_____

How can the story of Jairus' daughter inspire hope in situations that seem hopeless?

_____

_____

Who in your life needs encouragement or a reminder of Jesus' resurrection power? How can you be a source of that encouragement?

_____

_____

DECLARATION

In the face of despair and death, I will place my trust in Jesus, the Master of Life.

I believe He can and will bring restoration, healing, and revival to every area of my life.

DAY 25

A COMPASSIONATE INTERRUPTION

Luke 7:14-15 - *Then he walked over to the coffin and touched it, and the bearers stopped. 'Young man,' he said, 'I tell you, get up.' Then the dead boy sat up and began to talk! And Jesus gave him back to his mother.*

GOD SPEAK TO ME

Start by asking God to show His compassion in your life and the lives of those around you. Open your heart and mind to hear what God has to say to you today.

DEVOTIONAL

In the city of Nain, a sorrowful procession was taking place. A widow, already bereaved of her husband, was now facing the death of her only son. The weight of her grief was immeasurable. But as this somber scene unfolded, Jesus, moved with compassion, stepped into the midst of the mourners.

He didn't just sympathize from afar; He intervened with divine authority and compassion. With a touch and a command, He brought the widow's son back to life.

This miracle reveals Jesus' heart for the broken and grieving. It reminds us that He not only sees our pain but is moved to action on our behalf. No situation is beyond His reach, and His compassion is without limits.

SCRIPTURES TO READ

Luke 7:11-17; Psalm 34:18; 2 Corinthians 1:3-4

PRAYER OF RESPONSE

Dear Heavenly Father, thank You for your boundless compassion. I am grateful that You not only see my pain but also step into my situation with healing and hope. Let me reflect Your compassion to those around me. Amen.

SO WHAT? WHO CARES? HOW DOES THIS APPLY TO ME?

When have you felt the compassionate touch of Jesus in your life? Describe that moment.

_____

_____

How can you be a vessel of God's compassion to someone in need today?

_____

_____

Why is it important to remember that Jesus is not just a distant observer but an active participant in our lives?

_____

_____

How can the story of the widow's son at Nain encourage you or someone you know who is grieving?

_____

_____

How can you remind yourself daily of Jesus' compassion and love for you?

_____

_____

DECLARATION

In my moments of despair and sorrow, I will remember the compassionate touch of Jesus.

He is near to the brokenhearted and ready to bring restoration and healing. I will also be a bearer of His compassion to others.

DAY 26

DEFYING THE IMPOSSIBLE

Matthew 14:29 - *"Yes, come," Jesus said. So Peter went over the side of the boat and walked on the water toward Jesus.*

GOD SPEAK TO ME

Start by asking God to increase your faith and help you trust Him in the midst of life's storms. Open your heart and mind to hear what God has to say to you today.

DEVOTIONAL

The disciples were already in awe of Jesus feeding the 5,000 when they found themselves facing another astonishing display of His power. Caught in the midst of a storm, they see a figure walking on the tumultuous waves. Their initial fear is calmed when they realize it's Jesus. But then, Peter, impulsive as ever, requests to join Jesus on the water.

And for a moment, he does! Peter walks on water, a feat humanly impossible, defying the laws of nature. Yet, when his focus shifted from Jesus to the surrounding storm, he began to sink. This story serves as a powerful reminder that when our eyes are fixed on Jesus, we can achieve the seemingly impossible. But the moment our focus shifts to our circumstances, fear and doubt can creep in and sink us.

SCRIPTURES TO READ

Matthew 14:22-33; Hebrews 12:2; Isaiah 26:3

PRAYER OF RESPONSE

Dear Heavenly Father, help me to keep my eyes fixed on You, especially when I am surrounded by life's storms. Increase my faith, and let me be a testament to Your power and love. When I am overwhelmed, remind me of Your presence and Your ability to make the impossible possible. Amen.

SO WHAT? WHO CARES? HOW DOES THIS APPLY TO ME?

Have you ever experienced a moment when you felt like you were "walking on water" with Jesus? Describe it.

_____

_____

What "storms" in your life have caused you to shift your focus from Jesus?

_____

_____

How can you practically keep your eyes on Jesus during challenging times?

_____

_____

Why do you think Peter asked to walk on the water? What does this reveal about his relationship with Jesus?

_____

_____

How can you encourage someone today who might be sinking in their own "storm"?

_____

_____

DECLARATION

Even in the midst of chaos and uncertainty, I will keep my eyes fixed on Jesus, trusting in His power to help me navigate any challenge.

I am not defined by the storms but by my relationship with the One who walks on water.

DAY 27

MERCY IN MIDST OF CHAOS

Luke 22:51 - *But Jesus said, 'No more of this.' And he touched the man's ear and healed him.*

GOD SPEAK TO ME

Start by asking God to instill in you a heart of compassion and mercy, even towards those who might not understand or appreciate it. Open your heart and mind to hear what God has to say to you today.

DEVOTIONAL

The Garden of Gethsemane was a scene of high tension. Jesus was about to be betrayed, and His disciples were on edge. In a rash act, Peter drew his sword and struck the servant of the high priest, cutting off his ear. But in the midst of this chaos, Jesus demonstrated profound mercy. He healed Malchus' ear, showcasing His consistent love and compassion.

This act was a powerful testament to Jesus' character. Even when faced with betrayal and the looming crucifixion, He chose to heal rather than harm. It's a call for all of us to exhibit love and mercy, even in challenging circumstances, reflecting the character of our Savior.

SCRIPTURES TO READ

Luke 22:47-53; 1 Peter 2:21-23; Romans 12:17-21

PRAYER OF RESPONSE

Dear Heavenly Father, thank You for showing unmatched mercy even in Your most trying moments. Help me to respond with grace and love even when it's challenging. Let my actions reflect Your heart, choosing compassion over confrontation. Amen.

SO WHAT? WHO CARES? HOW DOES THIS APPLY TO ME?

How do you typically respond when faced with hostility or betrayal?

_____

_____

Why do you think Jesus chose to heal Malchus' ear in such a tense moment?

_____

_____

Can you recall a time when you chose mercy over retaliation? How did it make you feel?

_____

_____

How can you actively demonstrate Jesus' love to those who might oppose or misunderstand you?

_____

_____

Why is it essential for us, as followers of Christ, to show mercy even when it's undeserved?

_____

_____

DECLARATION

I will choose to act in love and mercy, reflecting the character of Jesus.

No matter the situation, I will strive to exhibit compassion, understanding that this is how God acts towards me daily.

DAY 28

DISTANCE MAKES NO DIFFERENCE

John 4:50 - *Then Jesus told him, 'Go back home. Your son will live!' And the man believed what Jesus said and started home.*

GOD SPEAK TO ME

Start by asking God to increase your faith in His omnipresence, understanding that He isn't limited by space or distance. Open your heart and mind to hear what God has to say to you today.

DEVOTIONAL

The nobleman's plea was urgent. His son was at the point of death. Yet, even when Jesus wasn't physically present at the boy's side, His word was enough to heal. This account isn't just a testament to Jesus' miraculous power but also a vivid illustration of the vast reach of His authority.

In our lives, sometimes God's answers may not come in the manner or timing we expect. But as this nobleman learned, faith is about trusting in Jesus' word, even when circumstances seem bleak. Our Savior's authority isn't restricted by time, space, or circumstance. His promises hold true, and His word never returns void.

SCRIPTURES TO READ

John 4:43-54; Isaiah 55:10-11; Matthew 8:5-13

PRAYER OF RESPONSE

Dear Heavenly Father, I thank You for Your unmatched power and authority. Teach me to trust in Your word, even when I can't see the immediate outcome. Help me to understand that You aren't bound by the limits of our physical world. Increase my faith in Your limitless capabilities. Amen.

SO WHAT? WHO CARES? HOW DOES THIS APPLY TO ME?

Can you recall a moment when God worked in an unexpected way in your life?

_____

_____

Why do you think Jesus chose to heal the nobleman's son without physically being there?

_____

_____

How does understanding Jesus' omnipresence change the way you approach prayer and faith?

_____

_____

What area in your life do you need to trust God more, even if you can't see the outcome yet?

_____

_____

How can you encourage someone today who might be struggling with trusting in God's timing and methods?

_____

_____

DECLARATION

I will trust in the word of Jesus, recognizing that His power and promises are not constrained by any limitations.

My faith is anchored in His omnipotent and ever-present nature.

DAY 29

WHEN THE UNEXPECTED BRINGS HEALING

2 Kings 5:14 - *So Naaman went down to the Jordan River and dipped himself seven times, as the man of God had instructed him. And his skin became as healthy as the skin of a young child, and he was healed!*

GOD SPEAK TO ME

Start by asking God to show you His unconventional ways of healing and restoration in your life. Open your heart and mind to hear what God has to say to you today.

DEVOTIONAL

Naaman, the Syrian army commander, was powerful, respected, and successful, but he had leprosy. An Israelite slave girl told him about the prophet Elisha, who could heal him. Expecting a grand spectacle, Naaman was disappointed when Elisha sent a messenger with simple instructions: bathe in the Jordan River seven times.

It was a test of humility for the proud commander. Reluctantly, he followed the instructions and was healed. This miracle reminds us that God's ways are not always our ways. Sometimes, God's method of healing or delivering may seem too simple, unconventional, or humbling, but it always leads to restoration.

SCRIPTURES TO READ

2 Kings 5:1-19; Isaiah 55:8-9; James 4:6-10

PRAYER OF RESPONSE

Dear Heavenly Father, help me to trust in Your ways, even when they don't align with my expectations. Remove any pride or preconceived notions, and let me be obedient to Your instructions, finding healing and restoration in You. Amen.

SO WHAT? WHO CARES? HOW DOES THIS APPLY TO ME?

Have you ever expected God to move in a specific way, only to be surprised by His approach? Describe the situation.

_____

_____

How does Naaman's initial reaction to Elisha's instructions resonate with your feelings when God's ways don't match your expectations?

_____

_____

How does humility play a role in experiencing God's miracles?

_____

_____

In what areas of your life do you need to let go of your expectations and trust God's unconventional methods?

_____

_____

How has God shown His power and love in unexpected ways in your life?

_____

_____

DECLARATION

I declare that God's ways are higher than my ways.

I will trust in His wisdom, seeking humility and obedience to experience His fullness and restoration in my life.

DAY 30

CHAIN BREAKER

Mark 9:25 - *When Jesus saw that the crowd of onlookers was growing, he rebuked the evil spirit. 'Listen, you spirit that makes this boy unable to hear and speak,' he said. 'I command you to come out of this child and never enter him again!'*

GOD SPEAK TO ME

Start by asking God to highlight areas of your life or loved ones who need deliverance and spiritual freedom. Open your heart and mind to hear what God has to say to you today.

DEVOTIONAL

A desperate father, a tormented son, and faith that seemed to waver — this is the backdrop for one of Jesus' most powerful miracles. When the disciples couldn't heal the boy, the father turned to Jesus with a mix of faith and doubt, saying, "if you can do anything, take pity on us and help us!" Jesus' response, "If you can?" emphasizes that all things are possible to those who believe.

In casting out the spirit, Jesus didn't just heal the boy physically; He delivered him spiritually. The chains that held him were broken. Jesus' power isn't limited by the challenges we face or the doubts we hold. It extends into the deepest recesses of our bondage, promising freedom and restoration.

SCRIPTURES TO READ

Mark 9:14-29; Luke 9:37-43; Ephesians 6:10-18

PRAYER OF RESPONSE

Dear Heavenly Father, You are the chain breaker and the deliverer. I bring before You every area of my life and those I love that are in need of Your touch. Strengthen my faith, and let me witness Your power as I trust in You for deliverance and healing. Amen.

SO WHAT? WHO CARES? HOW DOES THIS APPLY TO ME?

Have you ever felt like the father in the story, torn between hope and doubt? Describe the situation.

_____

_____

How does Jesus' assurance that all things are possible to those who believe resonate with you?

_____

_____

Are there areas in your life or someone you know that require spiritual deliverance?

_____

_____

How does this story reinforce the importance of persistent prayer and fasting?

_____

_____

What chains do you believe Jesus wants to break in your life or in the life of someone you care about?

_____

_____

DECLARATION

I declare that Jesus is my deliverer, and through Him, every chain can be broken.

I will believe and trust in His mighty power for freedom and healing in every area of my life.

Thank you for embarking on this 30 day transformative journey with us through the pages of this book. We hope that the devotionals, prayers and declarations have touched your heart and inspired you in profound ways. As we conclude this journey, we invite you to continue the conversation and connect with us further.

If you'd like to stay updated on our future endeavors, gain additional insights, and be a part of our vibrant community, we encourage you to follow us on social media. You can find us on most social media platforms like TikTok, Instagram, and Facebook by searching for our usernames:

@joewoodstuff

@nicolewoodtv

@theprayerfountain

We understand the power of prayer and the importance of supporting one another through life's challenges. If you have any prayer requests or would like to share your own spiritual journey, we invite you to visit our website:

 www.PrayerFountain.com.

This dedicated space is designed to create a sanctuary of hope and connection, where you can submit your prayer requests, receive prayer and pray for others.

Remember, life's journey is best walked together, hand in hand, supporting and uplifting one another along the way. We look forward to connecting with you, hearing your stories, and sharing in the power of prayer.

May your path be filled with God's unmerited favor, blessings, and uncommon success.

With heartfelt gratitude,

- Joe and Nicole Wood

Made in the USA
Columbia, SC
22 November 2024

47364487R00070